Thomas Boden

RIDE A WHITE HORSE

RIDE A WHITE HORSE

A Collection of Poems

Donna Boden

Copyright © 2003 by Donna Boden.

ISBN: Softcover   1-4134-2238-1

All rights reserved. No part of this book may be reproduced or transmitted in any form or by any means, electronic or mechanical, including photocopying, recording, or by any information storage and retrieval system, without permission in writing from the copyright owner.

This book was printed in the United States of America.

All Bible quotations are taken from the New King James Version

To order additional copies of this book, contact:
Xlibris Corporation
1-888-795-4274
www.Xlibris.com
Orders@Xlibris.com
20623

Acknowledgements

To my children and my husband who have
been such an encouragement to me, and the
Father God who truly rewards those
who diligently seek Him.

Donna Boden

FROM THE AUTHOR

The very earliest memories that I have are of communicating with God. I seem to have always had a knowledge of Him and His guidance in my life. At the early age of five I accepted Him as my Lord and Savior.

When I was eight the Lord visited with me in a dream, and gave me a vision of what I would be doing for Him in the later years of my life. When I was twelve He called me to be a missionary in a Sunday evening church service. From that time on I seemed to have had one purpose in my life; the call of God consumed me.

As a young adult I thought I lost the vision and plan of God, going my own way for a few years. When I returned to Him fully I was filled with remorse for what I perceived to be my messing up of His will for me.

In October of 1990 the Lord once again came to me. He took me, in a dream or vision, I do not know which, up on the top of a mountain and showed me a city and an area of the country. He asked me to go to that city and to pray for the people and to love them in His name. He further showed me that this was the mission field He had called me to when I was twelve and that in a few years this area would be known the world over with millions of people coming here every year. All of those years when I thought I had messed up His purpose for my life He was just developing in me the love and character of Jesus and preparing me for that which was to come to pass in and through me in the coming years; the final stage of my life here on earth.

These poems and psalms began to come to me in 1991. Most of them came to me while I was praying for others. Some of them are even prayers that I have prayed or sung over people, or groups of people, through the years.

My desire in sharing them with you is that they might be a blessing and an encouragement to you for your day to day walk.

Donna Boden

CONTENTS

~To The First Nations~

Ride A White Horse 14
Flight of the Chief 16
Man In The Flame 17
Blood Justice 18
Spirit Song 20
The Weaver 21
Crow Song 22
It is a Good Day to Die 24
She Who Walks With God 26

~ The Wonderful Creation of God~

The Waterfall 30
The Cardinal 31
Lesson of the Fawn 32
Protection of the Eagles 33
Graceful Butterfly 34
God's Garden 35
A Strand of Pearls 36
My Garden 37
Green Evergreen 38

~ The Fruit of The Spirit ~

God's Love 42
Rejoice 43
Peace 44
Trials 45
Faith 46
Mercy—Love—Grace 47
Forgiveness 48
Grace 49

~ Love of Families ~

A New Life (for my niece Emily) 52
Mother's Song 54
Little Bundle 55
Growing Up (A Mothers Love for her Daughter) 56
Mother's Home 57
Three Strand Cord 60
A Father's Heart 61

~ Intimacy With Him ~

Awakening 64
Essay From My Lord 65
Security 68
Longing 69
Ishi (Hebrew for husband) 70
God's Strength 72
My Soul 73
Your Glory 74
For You Alone I Sing 75
Hollow of God's Hand 76

~ Spirit of Revival and Harvest ~

Watchman 78

Holy Fire 79

Eagle Watch 80

River Of Glory 82

The House That God Built 84

Plow My Heart Oh God 86

Calvary's Way 88

~To The First Nations~

The poem **Ride a White Horse** was a direct result of a statement made by a man during the first "Day of National Prayer" in the Navajo Nation in 1998. He stated that it was time for the Navajo to "ride a new horse." As I began to pray for them to ride a new horse, the words of the poem came to me.

This section of poems is a dedication to the Native America People of North America. I believe very soon they will be pushed into a position of prominence in the realm of events occuring as this world comes into its final hour.

History records that in the advance and settlement of Europeans into the continent of North America, they didn't just try to conquer and rule the people already occupying the land, they tried to completely wipe them out. Satan tried to kill all the Native Americans to elimante those chosen of God.

There has been much research written on the North American Indians from as early as the 1500's stating that many of the tribes are truly of the "lost tribes of Israel." In talking to individuals in some of the tribes I found that, within the tribes themselves, many believe that they originated from tribes of Israel. My prayer is that God might bring to them the realization of the fullness of their heritage.

Donna

Ride A White Horse

Ride a white horse into battle
Chanting a loud victory song,
Ride with the Chief of all nations
Jesus the true Son of God.

Look, see the Spirits on Zion
Those who before you have gone,
Waving you on to the victory
Singing the Spirit's true song.

For way to long now, no seeing
Your eyes to God's truth were blind,
Satan's desire was . . . destroy all
The remnant that God sought to hide.

Now is the day of bright shinning
Today truth will out shine the lie,
Jesus in all of His Glory
Will ride a white horse by your side.

Go into battle with vigor
Fight Satan with all of your might,
Run with the Spirit Creator
Count coup . . . the true enemy dies.

Angels will go with the army
Eagles o're head they will fly,
God in His greatness and mercy
Will revive the Diné for the fight.

Break free of soul persecution
Look higher, a covenant cut,
The pure sinless blood of Jesus
It's always more than enough.

The enemy here is confined
To the realm of the soul and mind,
Your weapons of warfare aren't carnal
But mighty through God for all time.

Look, see the horses, they're pounding
Over the new war terrain,
The runners so close behind them
Victory is there for to gain.

So destroy all Satan's demons
Drive out the forces of hell,
Loose the Diné for the Glory
God's Holy Spirit to fell.

Freedom from bondage and darkness
Hope, truth, the light of the Son,
Filling your being with God's strength
For the last lap you now will run.

Ride a white horse into battle
Chanting a loud victory song,
Ride with the Chief of all nations
Jesus the true son of God!

Flight of the Chief

The old chief stood
His hands upraised
The sun did rise
In its fiery blaze

His body still
His soul at rest
His spirit soared
High as the eagle's nest

For many years
Life's path he'd walked
To lead his people
Near and far

In battle mighty
Husband, father, friend
His triumphant deeds
Sung time and again

The village quiet
While still at rest
As the morning dawn
Topped the mountain's crest

Then he saw
In the faint dawn light
The eagle climbing
For the morn's first flight

His old heart knew
Earth's journey o're
Before dawn's full light
He would close life's door

To fly high above
Where the Son does shine
Up to the Creator
Of all time

To the one he'd waited
Longing so to see
Who had guided him
Ever, diligently

His body still
His soul at rest
His spirit soared
Past the eagle's nest.

Man In The Flame

The flames leaped tall and bright
and then,
I saw within the flames a man;
upon a horse, his hands upraised
to give the Father song and praise.
I looked within the fire again,
and saw a lance beside the man.
He reached his hand,
and lifted high
a banner furled toward the sky.
I looked within the fire there
the horse did rear,
nostrils flared;
front hoofs pawing with all their might
most clearly ready for the fight.
The Son of God in all His splendor
when the heavens rend asunder,
will ride a horse of power and might
leading His army for the final fight.
The victory will most definitely go
to Him, for 2000 years ago
He paid the price and won the fight
He gave His body—
        blood, and life!

Blood Justice

The words were spoken ...
                they were said
When all was done ...
                many were dead.

The Lord looked down ...
                He heard a sound
Their blood was spilled ...
                crying from the ground.

The true people knew ...
                that rich red flow
Meant life and death ...
                on earth below.

When life was taken ...
                food to sustain
They were thankful ...
                for all it contained.

Fox, Rabbit, Fish, Bird ...
                Bear, Deer and Buffalo
The people honored ...
                that red blood flow.

But when it came . . .
        to the European man
He lost his sight . . .
        of God's great plan.

He spilled your blood . . .
        seemingly without a care
His Brothers, Sisters . . .
        how could he dare!

It seems as though . . .
        he could not see
Beyond the hatred . . .
        flowing fast and free.

Brothers, of my Fathers blood . . .
        forgive the white man's deed
For what to you was done . . .
        through malice, and greed.

Like Joseph who, long before . . .
        in suffering, wrong, and pain
Become a fine tuned servant . . .
        for your people's gain.

Lift high your eyes . . .
        look only to the light
Truth you'll surely see . . .
        God's most loving might.

Spirit Song

Spirit of the Sovereign God
Dance around the council fires,
Truth and light and life to show
To your remnant here below.

Sound the drum long and loud
Call the people gather round,
Wind and fire and rain to flow
Cleansing spirit, body, soul.

See the flame leap tall and bright
God in glory, power, and might,
Comes to those that He has called
To heal, renew both near and far.

Cherokee and Diné so strong
Sent as Joseph's sons belong,
Guiders of the way to life
The one true Son of God is right.

Come my children dance with me
Wind of the Spirit, oh so free,
Son of Righteousness to rise
With healing in His wings!

The Weaver

She sits at her loom
    her fingers nimble
Weaving in and out . . .
    . . . out and in.
Her threads are
    shinning colors.
No one knows,
    they cannot tell
What her finished
    work will be.
She weaves the
    . . . pictures
From her heart
They're a mirror
    of her soul!

Crow Song

Warriors

See the Crow fly free
See him soar upon the wind
See the Crow fly free
In the Spirit to ascend
See the Crow—fly free!

Mighty warriors tall
Mighty warriors strong
As they fly to battle
Others come along
As the Crow—flies free!

Hear the drum beat loud
Hear the drum beat strong
Hear the drum beat now
The Spirit's one true song
As the Crow—flies free!

See the chains break off
All the bondage gone
As he gazes on the Son
New freedom now is his
As the Crow—flies free!

It's a wondrous day
To only Jesus he belongs
To no other God
Will he ever bow again
As the Crow—flies Free!

Maidens

See the Crow fly free
See her soar upon the wind
See the Crow fly free
In the Spirit to ascend
See the Crow—fly free!

Let the maidens dance
In their feet a new song
Let the singers chant
Giving praise to God alone
As the Crow—flies free!

As the maidens dance
Colors flashing with each step
See their spirits soar
High past the eagle's nest
As the Crow—flies free!

Watch the maidens fly
May their voices be light
Singing to the Son of God
The way, The truth, The life
As the Crow—flies free!

See the Son of God smile
As He looks down to see
The Crow from bondage break
That has held her oh so long
As the Crow—flies free!

It is a Good Day to Die

Ride a white horse to battle
    holding high the war lance.
Spirit of the Holy One forward
    spirit of darkness to fall.
It is a good day to die!

Raise it up high, the banner
    call forth the sound battle cry.
Death to the enemy around us
    death to the flesh of the soul.
It is a good day to die!

Sing a new song of victory
    shout to the King of the Chiefs.
Dance to the Son of all Glory
    Holy Spirit Creator is here.
It is a good day to die!

Live a new life in the Spirit
    of ages before and to come.
Dance to Him, with all your being
    sing to the Lord a new song.
It is a good day to die!

There's a new language of speaking
   a new way of thinking to be.
Living newness of life in your being
   walking this path, for others to see.
It is a good day to die!

Seeing in spirit the High Priest
   waiting expectantly Him who will come.
Walking intimately with God the Creator
   running as none has before ever run.
It is a good day to die!

She Who Walks With God

She waits by the door
Her blood pounding hard
All her heart desires
Lays out and beyond
So near - yet so far.

Her dreams, her visions
Flowing all around her
As a bird inside a cage
Longing to fly - to go
Held by His unseen hand.

Her heart a bright treasure
Burning hot, fierce, high
Waiting for her direction
God's messenger servant
To help bring the Cherokee rest.

~ ~ ~ ~

Soon now - yes soon
And she will be free
To bring His chosen people
To the true light to see
The beauty of their Lord.

Scattered, hidden so long ago
From hills to long away shores
So deep in God's mystery
That even their enemy
Did not fully see, or know..

Now, at the end of the ages
The God of all will renew
His chosen remnant
So close to His heart
Ever under His holy eye.

~ ~ ~ ~

So now she stands
To begin the completion
Poised at the ready
Of a mystery of God
A crown for Jesus feet.

To bring forth a people
So long trodden down
To the bright light
Of their birthright
To the joy of the Son.

The brightness of His glory
Truth His people to show
A way to the true God
For hundreds of years
They just did not know.

~ ~ ~ ~

Arise now, oh daughter
Who walks with God
Blow a trumpet of Zion
Those so precious to Him
His kingdom to show.

And nations will turn
In an hour and a day
From sin and deception
To the God of their ancients
The Holy Ghost's power.

To know who they really are
Protected always from afar
Brought forth into unity
In this final hour - to stand
With their brethren for right.

~ ~ ~ ~

Oh Israel, My mercy's at hand
Over the waters a remnant will stand
To help you — sustain you
And feed you aright — your brothers
Arising, in My power and might.

They will sing forth My praise
Through the day and all night
They will dance around fires
A new song in their hearts,
True freedom known at last.

Those American Nations
Called Indians by white
Downtrodden no longer
Will know in these last days,
Their heritage birthright!

~The Wonderful Creation of God~

Then God saw everything that He had made, and indeed it was very good.

So the evening and the morning were the sixth day.

Thus the heavens and the earth, and all the host of them, were finished.

And on the seventh day God ended His work which He had done, and He rested on the seventh day from all His work which He had done.

Genesis 1:31-2:2

The Waterfall

I sit beneath the waterfall
        to watch the tumbling spray.
Glistening water drops of light
        to flow along its way.

I sit beneath the waterfall
        to hear the music sweet.
Water over smoothest stones
        to a pool so very deep.

I sit beneath the waterfall
        to feel the coolest spray.
Mist so fine upon my face
        to bathe, then melt away.

I sit beneath the waterfall
        drinking water oh so sweet.
Its coolness will quench my thirst
        to keep 'til next we meet.

I sit beneath the waterfall
        to hear Jesus gently say,
Bring others here in prayer to Me
        to find My truth, My life,
              . My way!

The Cardinal

A cardinal lit upon a branch
outside my windowsill.
He cocked his head
and looked about,
but all was calm and still.
I heard him chirp,
he turned his head
first right, then left and right
just then I saw his counterpart
fly past, and then alight.
Her color, not so bright and grand
as his, but then I found
while she did eat the seed nearby
my eyes on him were bound.
Iridescent red, oh so bright
the sun on him did shine,
I hardly even noticed her
'twas on him I had my mind.
As I gazed,
my thought took flight
to my Father in heaven above
who watches over you and me
guarding us with eternal love.
If we let His Son, within—
our hearts,
and then our lives
when others look, they'll only see
the Son in us—does shine!

Lesson of the Fawn

This morning
    in the early dew
A deer and fawn
    came into view
They ran and jumped
    frolicking about
Their Love exchanged
    there was no doubt
I couldn't help
    but think again
About the Love
    that God did send
He'd have us run
    and leap and fall
Into His arms
    to Love us all!

Protection of the Eagles

The Eagles fly with
    outstretched wing
Their eyes trained
    to the earth below,
When they let go
    with God's word
The Angels see
    it's done just so.

When the missiles
    from the earth
Towards them
    they do fly,
The Angels just
    deflect their flow
Into the wide
    blue sky.

Graceful Butterfly

A butterfly is precious
Its beauty we can see,
Freely flying here to there
The world its splendor to behold.
Lest we forget, let's look and see
Where did this beauty come,
From months of laying quietly
Woven tightly in a silken mold.

If we'd have our spirit be
As the gentle butterfly,
A precious thing of beauty
To soar and dip and freely fly.
We must submit our will to God
Spend time in our cocoon,
Filling there our heart and mind
With His Spirit and His Truth.

Then and only then will we
Be ready here and there to fly,
So others may behold and see
What God has made so beautiful.
Freely we've been given grace
Surely we have received,
Freely we should share that grace
To those who are in need.

God's Garden

There's a fragrance in the land
    It is pleasing to My Son
A Holy smell of roses
    And jasmine in the night.

The prayers of My people
    Who give up their own way
To be a willing vessel
    To speak My word aright.

So the fragrance, oh so pleasing
    As the will is pressed to yield
Spilling forth the oil of healing
    By My hand, power, and might.

From this Holy fragrant garden
    That I groomed and pruned just so
Spills the fragrance that I honor
    My pray-ers lives, a Living Light.

A Strand of Pearls

'Tis just a tiny grain of sand
worked in the oyster by God's plan
and through His way and time, it can
become a valued pearl for man.
Into your life flows this grain of sand
across your path, by His dear plan
and with your prayers to Him, it can
become that valued pearl for man.
In His eyes they're precious see
sands of the purest specialty
cared and polished, just so—
                      by Him,
by His Spirit they become His Gem.
So when you bow your head to pray
God's word over them each day
though others may not know, or see
He creates a strand of pearls—
                      by thee.
Washed in the Lamb's sinless blood
Filled with the Spirit, sweetest wine
guided in their lives, day by day
Because God reached through you,
                      to pray!

My Garden

I look around and then I see
    the Glory of You in a tree.

I listen to the sounds and hear
    a bird that sings so true and clear.

A flower, tree, or fruit I touch
    and know Your love is ever much.

The wind does blow so I can smell
    the fragrance from a flower fell.

I pick a fruit that I may taste
    and know all this You Lord did make.

Green Evergreen

The green trees are laden
with heavy snow.
Their branches are low laying
from the weight of that snow.
The wind, gently at first
then harder
blows the snow off the branches.
If the wind blows to hard at first
the branches would surely break.
The wind blows the snow
everywhere!
The green trees, the live trees
swaying in the wind.
You are a green tree
a living green tree.
Even in the winter of your life
God sends the snow
to cover you, with moisture
so that
you are laden down with the weight;
the Glory of the Lord—
         His snow.

Ask His Holy Spirit to blow
His breath upon your branches
gently, then more fiercely
swirling His Glory all around you.
People—Marriages
Places—Businesses
Prayer, Praise, Worship
covered with the light of His Glory.
It is an eternal well
of Glory
He has filled you up completely.
By your willingness to be broken
He has prepared your heart for Him.
He has gentled you.
Now He
can pour His Glory through you
Into the lives of others!

~ The Fruit of The Spirit ~

But the fruit of the Spirit is love, joy, peace, longsuffering, kindness, goodness, faithfulness, gentleness, self-control. Against such there is no law.

Galatians 5:22-23

God's Love

I sat today
    and looked about
At all the things
    that I could count,
The trees, the sky
    the birds, and all
That God has made
    and placed around,
So we could see
    His loving care
In everything that
    He placed there,
And we could know
    without a doubt
His love will always
    be poured out,
Upon our lives
    in rich array
To walk us through
    each and every day!

Rejoice

Each morning as I rise
I think
About the love God has
For me
It's there around me
Everywhere
In earth, and sea, and sky.
I can do naught except
Rejoice
In every single day,
In all of that which
My Father's
Loving hands have made!

Peace

One night I stayed up late, and then
I saw the stars that God did bend
To make the shapes for us to see
So we could know His majesty.

And in the knowing we would find
A peace, not of this earthly kind
A peace so sure, steadfast, and true
We never need to walk in fear.

Trials

When trials come
    they seem so hard,
The thunder rolls
    the raindrops fall.
The pain intense
    the daylight dim,
We only know
    to trust in Him.

But once the Son
    has broken through,
We see the rain
    as only dew.
And know for sure
    His loving care,
Has once again
    been proven there.

Faith

I sought for faith
I looked—
    I searched
Its treasure to behold.

But faith my friend
Cannot be found
For faith—
    is only grown!

Mercy—Love—Grace

Oh what a sinner I would be
        But for the Grace of God to me,
The motivation for His plan
        Was Love of God above for man.
With compassion He said, it's done
        And Mercy sent His only Son,
To hang and die upon a tree
        To sanctify both you and me.

I look to God today and say
        The Grace you gave I'll give away,
With all my Love for your dear Son
        I'll share with all what you've begun.
Your Mercy from my lips I'll send
        Not judgment on my fellow man,
Lord for your Mercy, Love, and Grace
        Within my life I'll make a place.

Forgiveness

I came to God in prayer and cried
    O Lord, I've sinned today.
He answered me in tender love
    Your sins I wash away.

Oh Lord, I cried, you do not see
    The scars are deep and wide.
I see, He said, so I may heal
    Your scars are proof I died.

Oh Lord, I think you do not know
    What will other people say?
I care not what they may think
    I've forgiven you this day.

I do not know, O Lord My God
    If myself I can forgive.
You'd best my child, for if you don't
    Your anguish will be real.

The path for you is easy now
    You just accept My grace,
Then let My love flow over you
    And walk in ways made straight.

Grace

I prayed this morning then I saw
The sacrifice of Grace was all
That I today would have or need
To be the one He'd have me be.

I prayed and looked again to see
One nailed by Grace upon a tree
His love stretched up to Heaven High
His arms stretched out to those nearby.

I prayed a third time and I knew
The Grace of God was only through
The death of one so innocent
That every sin I could repent.

As I bow and pray today
Grace from God will make my way
And when the evening I do see
I'll know the Grace of God kept me.

~ Love of Families ~

Then God said, "Let Us make man in Our image, according to Our Likeness"...So God created man in His own image; in the image of God He created him; male and female He created them. Then God blessed them, and God said to them, "Be fruitful and multiply; fill the earth and subdue it"...

Genesis 1:26-28

A New Life
(for my niece Emily)

A tiny life has been conceived
And now begins to grow
Will the babe be He or She
Soon now, and we will know.

In only weeks tiny little feet
And hands will start to move
Those very first light flutters
So precious they'll be to you.

The sonogram, oh what a sight
As you gaze upon his form
So tiny nestled there inside
Protected, safe, and warm.

Enjoy this time dear Emily
Treasure every day and hour
You baby snuggles in your womb
So active, yet so quiet now.

When the day of birth arrives
Amidst your pain and struggle
You'll bring a tiny baby forth
To hold in your arms and snuggle.

Remember always to gently train
Through the rights and wrongs of life
This little one that God deposited
Into your life one night.

Through the joyous times you'll laugh
Through the sorrows you will cry
For time will bring you some of both
As you travel through your life.

When it all is said and done
You'll look back across the years
And remember as though yesterday
The birth of your first born!

Mother's Song

Hello dear baby in my womb
You'll learn to know my voice real soon,
To know my touch, my smell, my feel
Above all others mine will be real.
For now, just rest and grow real strong
So soon the day will come along,
When I will give birth to you
Yes, we'll see each other soon.
I'll love you always is my promise
Know that as life upon you pulls,
There is no love like the love of Mother
There is no other bond so sure.
Oh Baby in my womb—my heart
I can hardly wait for our life to start,
For now I'll talk and sing to you
Then soon hold you in my arms too!

Little Bundle

Little feet to patter
    all across the floor,
Little hands to hold
    onto forevermore.

Little eyes to see
    what you will show,
Little ears to hear
    all that you know.

Babies are a Blessing
    sent from Heaven above
To have, to hold, to smother
    with all of your Love!

Growing Up
(A Mother's Love for her Daughter)

Growing up
  sometimes...
    seems hard
For stretching takes
your very all.
But once
you're grown
and looking back,
You'll see the
  Love
    we always had.
And though...
  at times it
seemed so small,
You'll know
  Love
helped you...
  through it all!

Mother's Home

Others looked at her and said
She did little for God at all
She rarely went outside her home
Or even got involved.

Then a child that she had raised
Stepped forth to loud proclaim
You do not know, so I will tell
God's way was her one aim.

Her adornment was'nt outward
In hair and dress so fine
To see it you had to look
At her children's lives, see mine.

A pure heart hidden deep within
Incorruptible was her beauty
Her gentle, and peaceful spirit
Was so precious to us, truly.

Our home was always heated
By the warmth of her embrace
By that warmth each day we'd go
To run life's fast filled pace.

Her floors she swept and polished
With the word of God each day
We knew she dwelled with Jesus
As she filled each day with Praise.

The air she kept permeated
With Peace from God within
It filled the rooms with fragrance
We knew with whom she'd been.

Food aplenty on our table
Was as manna from Heaven above
She fed it to us daily
God's Wisdom, Grace, and Love.

Our weaknesses she covered
With her prayers so tenderly
Giving us the best example
So we learned of God's Mercy.

There was naught we could not tell her
She listened to our cries
Then soothed us with her wisdom
We knew she was on our side.

No matter what we did or said
She would see the good in us
Thus we could walk in confidence
Her love for us enough.

So Mothers look at your house
Ask of yourself today
What kind of home am I building
Is it an oasis from life's way?

Will your children call you Blessed
Knowing at the end of each day's stress
They will find a home that's filled with
Peace, Sweet Mercy, Grace and Rest!

Three Strand Cord

Sisters are bound by a cord
stronger than adversity
invisible to the human sight.
At times, by life's demands
stretched tight to almost breaking.
It remains
an anchor created by God
placed before time began
to hold together two precious lives.
Nourished by love,
a three strand cord—
two sisters and their maker.
Through family ties this cord
will not easily break, though
tested by the circumstances of life.
So let what God has united
by no earthly man be divided;
and, though Satan like a lion roars
no weapon will be found
that can break this invisible cord
so tightly woven, by God the creator
uniting two sisters into One.

A Father's Heart

A Father's heart
    is always open
        to his children;
His hand is there
    to give support
        along their way.
A Father's eyes
    are watching over
        their situations;
His feet to guide
    their steps
        as best he may.
So his children may
    walk confidently
        through their lives;
Knowing Daddy's
    very being will
        be their strength,
To lean upon
    as needed
        each and every day!

~ Intimacy With Him ~

*Before I formed you in the womb I knew you;
Before you were born I sanctified you; . . .*

Jeremiah 1:5

Awakening

Fingers gently touch my face
    warm sunlight to bathe me,
Waking me with loving call
    to the wondrous beauty of a day.

Choruses of music, oh so sweet
    to my hearing the songbirds sing,
Calling me to rise and enjoy
    the wondrous beauty of my day.

The flowers burst with fragrance
    perfuming the very atmosphere,
Everywhere my senses are embraced
    with the wondrous beauty of the day.

I thank you Lord for waking me
    with touch and voice and smell,
To all that you for me have made
    oh, the wondrous beauty of this day!

Essay From My Lord

Before the earth was
I formed you
I made you in my image.
When the appointed time came
I placed you within a human womb.
Before your Mother
ever heard your voice
I called you by My name.
To Me, you were a delight.
Before you could walk
I led you
I guided your paths.
Before you could talk
I directed your thoughts;
I sang to you—
    My Angels
sang to you
you knew the sound of My voice.

Within your family
you grew,
you became your own person
your will developed strong.

You became a personality,
with desires
and ways to go, designed by you.
I watched you
become an individual person
stretching to achieve the plans
that you had made.
Within your own family
you walked the path of life.
Growing to maturity
in the natural self of—
    soul and body.

In your Spirit
you worshiped Me;
lifting you voice and heart
you gave Me adoration.
You talked,
and walked with Me.
With your Spirit
you yeilded your will to
My will, laying down
your desires to follow Me.
You sang and
    danced for Me;
giving to Me freely

of yourself, your time,
your life.

You always looked for me,
in people, places,
and in every living thing
you knew that I had made.

So now—
    we'll walk this
life together.
Fellowshipping with
each other
and those I send your way.
You'll see things My way
saying, what you hear Me say
doing, what you see Me do.
So now
I give to you wisdom.
I give unto you richly
bringing you My anointing;
My power.
I declare you are a treasure.
You are pleasing to My Father
you are a pleasure unto Me!

Security

I woke amid the thunder
I watched the lighting flash
The rain fell hard in torrents
The wind blew branches past.

I thought about my Father
Who made the earth and sky
I thought of all His power
As I watched the storm blow by.

The lightening broke the darkness
The thunder roared with sound
The rain filled all the air
The wind surely did abound.

The Son of God breaks darkness
God's voice like thunder roars
The Spirit rains within my soul
And blows through my heart door.

The Lord in all His Splendor
To us who are earthly bound
Can be a loving shelter
Where fear no more is found.

Longing

I longed today to go and see
      My Father in the Heavenlies
I wanted only to behold
      The face and touch of whom I know.

You cannot come, He said to me
      But if you'll look around you'll see
My face is carved in every man
      My touch in all upon the land.

It is enough, I said to Him
      It will sustain me now, and when
You think my life here to be through
      I'll then come home to live with you.

Ishi
(Hebrew for husband)

I serve the wonderful Son of all Glory
Power, and might—soon coming King
I serve the Lord of all creation
Captain of Heaven's armies
And I call him—Ishi!

There is found no other like Him
So wondrous—His great majesty
No power can come close to His
Though I search through eternity's time
Yet to me He is always, Ishi!

Come people, come bow before Him
Bow down and worship with me
The beautiful lamb, who was for sin slain
The conquering King of the ages
My savior, my master,—Ishi!

Arrayed—He's arrayed in great splendor
His bridal clothes spotless and fine
His countenance shines through all darkness
I will sing of His love—forever
Oh Ishi, oh Ishi, he's mine!

His blood courses all through my body
Healing spirit, emotions, and mind
His breath, so fragrant and pleasing
His presence penetrates through all of time
Oh Ishi, my master, my lover!

I come to Him clothed in fine garments
With diamonds and pearls shining bright,
My face, my hair shine with His light
His love is so completely mine
Oh Ishi, my husband, my life!

God's Strength

I thought today, oh Lord I'll walk
Both straight and tall, I'll give my all
I'm stronger Lord today you see
Within my strength I'll walk for thee.

I went about a mile and then
Flat on my face, I fell again
I could not understand just why
For truly Lord I really tried.

Gently then He spoke to me
My child, your strength I do not need
In your weakness I'm made strong
It's My strength carries you along.

I think tomorrow Lord I'll try
To walk ever closer, by your side
For with your strength flowing through me
I'll be all Lord you'd have me be.

My Soul

I bring my will today to you
And lay it at your feet
'Tis all I have to give you Lord
My will I give to thee.

I bring my emotions to you Lord
And lay them at your feet
I found there is more than my will
My emotions I give to thee.

I bring my mind to you today
And lay it at your feet
My will, emotions, mind, oh Lord
My Soul I give to thee.

Your Glory

My flesh today I crucify
Within my flesh I cannot walk

My soul today, I will renew
For by your word alone I speak

My spirit Lord, will lead the way
That others might Your Glory see.

For You Alone I Sing

I sat today and wondered why
That God so big up in the sky
Did take time from His busy life
To make a person such as I

And then I saw a loving Lord
The three-in-one all in accord
Who wanted only what we desire
Someone to love and do things for

I sat today and said to God
Just let me love a little back
And if my life can mean a thing
Let it be for You alone I sing.

Hollow of God's Hand

I held a tiny tadpole
in the palm of my right hand.
It swam in shallow water there
secure within my palm.
I thought of how our Father
in Heaven high above
holds us in the hollow of
His hand
just as my small tadpole.
We are safe, secure, at peace,
no troubles can be found
it's only when we leave his hand
that pressures do abound.
Oh Lord, if we could but find
the way to walk each day
within the hollow of
Your hand
in peace and joy to stay.

~ Spirit of Revival and Harvest ~

Then He said to His disciples, "The harvest truly is plentiful, but the laborers are few. Therefore pray the Lord of the harvest to send out laborers into His harvest."

Matthew 9:37, 38

Watchman

To be a watchman standing tall
At my post, day and night on call
A watchman for my Lord to be
Holy Spirit please watch through me

A watchman answering the call
Watching over saints, God's children all
To be a watchman don't you see
Was what God created me to be

Looking in the Spirit realm to see
Then coming to Father, on bended knee
Pleading for those who know not how to
Standing in agreement with those who do

A watchman for my Lord I'll be
Honoring His sacrifice at Calvary
I'll watch and pray each day for you
As the Holy Spirit leads me to do!

Holy Fire

Holy fire from Heaven
 burn across this earth today
Leave us only ashes white,
 charred stumps of blackened clay.

Holy rain from Heaven
 rain on earth today
Ignite the small dead seeds
 under ashes they quietly lay.

Holy Spirit from Heaven
 raise up your Prophets now
Fill their mouths with your words
 proclaiming the coming power.

Apostles lead the people
 from ashes and clumps of clay
To become the wine filled vessels
 that Jesus did proclaim.

It was at the wedding supper
 He turned the water into wine
Within the clay, a miracle
 God's eternal love did shine.

It's written in the scriptures
 we are vessels made of clay
Oh Jesus, turn us into finest wine
 for this very hour and day!

Eagle Watch

An eagle sits atop the crag
head held high
watching . . .
silently searching,
Old Eagle Eye.
What does he see setting there
so stout, so brave
neither fearful
nor intimited,
only watchful.
Suddenly with swift uplift
he soars into the air
screeching . . .
wings uplifting
downward flow.
Where is he going
like a lightening flash
across the sky,
then shooting
to earth below.
To rise again with
uplifted wing
in his talons a
given token, of
his dive to earth.

What can we from
	the eagle learn.
		to sit . . .
		a watchful
		crag on high.
Watching in the Spirit
	through the Holy Spirit
		for just what
		we know
		not, for sure.
When catching a glimpse
	of earthy trouble
		we swiftly
		from our perch,
		take flight.
Darting with the swiftness
	of the eagle
		to snatch . . .
		the foe from
		mischief making.
In fervent intercession
	we lift him away
		from causing
		harm to
		God's dear child.
An eagle is a watcher
	a pray-er is the same
		ever seeing . . .
		in the Spirit,
		God's Watch Tower!

River Of Glory

There's a river of Glory
 and it is rising
It starts deep in the valley
 of our souls.
A river of God's Glory
 that is rising
Oh—now to overflow.

And let the people come
 let them run and jump
Let them swim and splash
 into the Glory.
This Glory of your soul
 from the Heavenly
Throne of God.

I am filling the earth
 with My Glory
That is rising from
 the valley of your soul
Glory, Holy, Glory
 Holy, Glory, Holy.

So Let the people come
    let them run and jump
Let them swim and splash
    into the Glory
This Glory of your soul
    from the Heavenly
Throne of God

All in My Glory,
    all in My Glory,
Let them laugh and sing
    let them, lead them,
Join them, in the river
    of My Glory

My Glory,
    from your very soul
It's overflowing
    to all the peoples
Tribes, and nations
    My Holy Glory.

The House That God Built

There is a house
  in the side of a hill
    it's built by love, it's built of Me.
There is a house
  of love to see
    and all who come will be filled by Me.
There is a house
  where love is found
    it's hidden now from beginning of time.
Now in this day
  and in this hour
    the road is there but few will find.
The fragrance fills
  the hills so sweet
    a pure perfume straight out of Me.
And those who know
  who look and see
    will be consumed of love from Me.
There is a house
  in the side of the rock
    tucked there by Me, the door not locked.
Look child and see
  this house today
    I built it up in My own way.

No other hand
    has had a say
        your house is solid, love is the way.
The path that leads
    those to your door
        is filled with Holy fragrance, evermore.
There is a house
    it's built by Me
        to all who come, My love they'll see.
So pray they find
    the path, the way
        to My house of love this hour, this day.
There is a house
    My love, My life
        no other way will stand earth's strife.
Oh children come
    and let Me be
        a house of love through you for Me.
The pathway find
    of love's pure light
        please light their path to Jesus tonight.

Plow My Heart Oh God

I went in spring to till the ground
I found it hard, I found it sound
I took a fork and I did make
A furrow long, a furrow straight
I fertilized with all my might
Then plowed it under for the night
So it might set until the rain
Would make it ready for the grain.

I planted seed and still did wait
So that the seed might germinate
The sun did shine and to my sight
The weeds did sprout, oh what a fright
I pulled and tugged, I hoed and then
I saw my seed sprout forth and send
A shoot, a stalk, both tall and straight
I hoed again loose soil to make.

Again the rain, the sun, the wind
To blow the pollen forth and send
And now my planting took a shape
If filled with fruit and on a date
In the future near I knew that now
What I had planted and I plowed
Would fill me and would satisfy
That for which I long had cried.

Let a lesson here be found
What we have sown into the ground
Of our heart and our mind
Will come a fruit that others find
Will it be weeds that God must pull
Or fruit of His Spirit flowing full
This day my will determines that
My heart I plow so that He might,

Fertilize and plow and then
Send the rain, the sun, the wind
For in the sending of His rain
My seed does sprout and create grain
I want a stalk both tall and straight
So fruit He might then start to make
That He might hoe my heart again
Sending more sun, rain, and wind.

To blow the pollen forth to send
More germination once again
That my life might begin to shape
into the image He would make
A shoot, a stalk that looks just like
The Son of God in power and might
And others might sweet fruit enjoy
For which they long have waited!

Calvary's Way

There was a man called of God
    stood at the foot of Calvary
His savior he did see.
He bowed his head
    and kneeled down low
At his Saviors feet.

Then Jesus reached down low
    and lifted him up high.
I brought your here son
He did say
    to show you My blood
Of Calvary's way.

My people on the earth
    the ones I love so much
Are dying and going to hell.
They are so blind—
    they cannot see
The truth of the blood of Calvary.

I need your hands—your eyes
    your voice
To tell them of my blood.
I need you to speak
    to tell the world
Of My most loving touch.

They search in places all so wrong
    they cry—they seek my peace.
If they would only turn and find
It's flowing in My river free,
    through My precious blood
Of Calvary.

That blood—
    that cleansing, healing flow
Oh that My people
Of earth should know.
    I paved the road
It's covered in my blood.

They cower, they hide
    they run in fear.
I want to clasp them ever near
To bring them into
    My bosom see,
And ever keep them close to Me.

I long to show My love
    forgiveness—that cleansing red
The precious blood for them I shed.
If you will speak
    then many will see
My saving blood of Calvary!

And if you'll look to only Me
    I'll give you visions of
The fullness of My blood.
Then give you words to say
    so you may show, the world
The blood of Calvary's way.